Table of content

	Page
Introduction	2
Chapter 1: The Merging of Traditional and Contemporary Elements	3
Chapter 2: Recipes for Holiday Breakfasts and Brunches	6
Chapter 3: Ideas for a Traditional Christmas Feast	9
Chapter 4: Eight Delicious Substitutes for the Traditional Christmas Feast	12
Chapter 5: You'll find 9 scrumptious and simple dessert recipes here	16
Chapter 6: Recipes for Festive Beverages	19
Chapter 7: "The Christmas Feast" Holiday Appetizers and Snacks	22
Chapter 8: Dealing with a Variety of Nutritional Requirements	25
Chapter 9: Advanced Study Methods Hints & Helpful Advice	28
Chapter 10: Five Options That Are Suitable for Children	31
Recipes	33
Stuffing with bacon for the holiday of Christmas	34
Fig And Orange Glazed Ham	38
Chestnuts, pancetta, and Brussels Sprouts with Parsley and Pancetta	41
Gratin d'Onions Crème fraîche	44
Carrot Cake	48
Ruby Red Velvet Cake	50
Sugar Cookies	52
Chocolate Caramel Candy	55
Homemade peanut butter cups	58
Conclusion	60

Introduction

People's moods throughout the holiday season could be affected by the act of cooking.

Possibly a confluence of causes is at play here. Our anticipation of the holiday season is heightened by the tantalising smells and tastes that accompany the season's many festive meals. But this puts a heavy burden on the shoulders of the chief cook in the house.

Most of the difficulties of holiday cooking can be avoided by taking a minimalist approach.

The truth is that we tend to make the production of food for the holidays more difficult than it needs to be by preparing too much food, too many different types of food, and not including the family in the process to assist lessen the host's work in the kitchen.

Chapter 1: The Merging of Traditional and Contemporary Elements

It is essential to preserve and pass on the traditions of one's family as much as possible. Even so, the adventure of exploration never disappoints. If you find out that no one in your family appreciates what you were doing, you should stop doing it. There's no reason to keep doing it just because it was done in the past.

Many dishes are appropriate to serve at a Christmas celebration, and many of them are rooted in tradition, but you can also add other dishes that are more up-to-date to give the event a more contemporary air.

Let's examine some tried-and-true recipes, and then talk about ways to update the menu:

1. In many cultures, Christmas parties wouldn't be complete without potato salad. This dish can easily be adapted to fit a variety of occasions. There are numerous approaches to taking this on

Why not try something new if you've always done it a certain way? If, for example, you always make a potato salad that is doused in mayonnaise, you may try making one that does not include mayonnaise for a change of pace.

2. Turkey It may sound unusual, but not everyone eats turkey on Christmas. Now more than ever, there is a demand for variety in the vegan food market, as many people in modern society have discovered the many health benefits of a plant-based diet.

Some people are just tired of having to go through the same motions year after year. Instead of the usual pasta or chicken, why not try something new, like the Mexican holiday favourite,

3. Chiles en Nogada.

The Feast of the Seven Fishes is the name given to this tradition, which has its roots in Italy.

Your holiday celebration can still be traditional while still being open to new ideas if you shift the emphasis of the event to reflect your own beliefs and practices.

4. Doro Wat on Injera, as it is well called, is the traditional Ethiopian Christmas supper.

It's a very spicy chicken stew. This recipe would work just as well with turkey as it would with chicken, and it would be a great way to use up leftover turkey from a traditional Thanksgiving meal. Blending the modern with the historical would be a brilliant and original idea.

Do what the Germans do: Many renowned culinary traditions can be found in Germany.

Instead of the traditional Thanksgiving turkey, why not try roasting a duck this year? Incorporating this into your Christmas meal is a good way to mix things up while still keeping with the holiday's traditional trappings.

In terms of nourishment, you understand the big picture. Think about your ancestry. It would be a lot of fun to do a DNA test to see where you come from and then have everyone at the holiday gathering bring a dish from the country they discovered they have ancestry from. Doing something like this with loved ones is always a good idea.

5. Create a Facebook group with your extended family around Halloween to talk about holiday recipes and the results of any DNA testing that has been done. Regardless of the path you choose, know that you have support. You can customise the process by choosing from a variety of available options, including getting help, skipping steps, and adding new ones.

Chapter 2: Recipes for Holiday Breakfasts and Brunches

Breakfast or brunch for a large group on Christmas Day? You might find it beneficial to browse the web for some food ideas. Don't forget, though, that a Christmas morning meal is not obligatory. This is something you may do whenever the holiday season strikes your fancy. If you expect a large group of people to spend Christmas morning at your home, it's a good idea to stock up on grab-and-go breakfast foods like muffins, doughnuts, and cereal.

Recipes for casseroles that can be made the night before - These are perfect for a quick and easy morning meal that will satisfy everyone's appetite.

These ten casserole recipes range from savoury to sweet and are all easy to make and delicious to eat. Don't be afraid to make changes to these suggestions if you find that you can't eat or don't like a certain ingredient in the recipe.

1. Rapidly Accessible Nutrition - Unwrapping presents and thinking about what has to be done before dinner is served are common morning activities. So, if you like, you may set out a variety of finger foods so that people can eat whenever they want to start as soon as they wake up.

2. Pop-tarts, oats, individual quiches, muffins, and even individual quiches are all good options for a Christmas brunch menu. Bake some cinnamon rolls in a pan shaped like a Christmas tree, then decorate them with red, green, gold, and silver sprinkles to show off your creative side.

3. The ham you received for Christmas can be enjoyed for breakfast. Rolls, spiralized ham, chutney, and other condiments are great additions to a ham dinner. The ability to make one's own is a right of every person. All you have to do is lay out the ham, rolls, and maybe some fruit and let them serve themselves.

4. A breakfast quiche is a great option because it can be prepared quickly yet still provides a filling meal. You can put anything you want into a quiche; the possibilities are endless. Individual quiches prepared in a muffin tray are an alternative if you need to feed a large group of people for breakfast who have different dietary needs (such as vegans). Keep in mind that Costco offers premade mini-quiches as well.

5. Bread Pudding - Make bread pudding for breakfast if you like. The process can be started the night before and completed first thing in the morning. Usually, this is correct. Serve this blueberry-pecan pancake bread pudding during Christmas brunch in place of the usual breakfast dishes for a more celebratory meal.

6. I'm Leaving the House to Eat Breakfast Going out for breakfast may seem counterintuitive at first, but it can end up saving you a lot of time and effort in the long run. Many restaurants will be open for brunch on Christmas Day. Going out for breakfast instead of the traditional lunch or dinner can be a lot of fun, and there are probably some great options in your neighbourhood that you can check out before heading to the movies.

7. Never Forget to Deliver the Knockout Punch! Christmas breakfast would be perfect with a special adult-only punch to celebrate the season.

You may make any kind of Christmas punch you desire; if you want a great recipe for Bloody Mary punch, check out Martha Stewart's website.

You can host a Christmas brunch on Christmas Eve, Christmas Day, or the day after Christmas; it doesn't matter. Whatever you'd like to make for Christmas brunch would be fine with me. Sharing scrumptious cuisine with those you care about is the essence of living.

Chapter 3: Ideas for a Traditional Christmas Feast

Inspiration is something that everyone can appreciate sometimes. The internet has made it much easier to discover new sources of motivation. There's no harm in calling up mom or grandma for a dose of motivation, even if the answer to your question is available online.

You shouldn't ignore any magazines, books, relatives, or friends who might have some fresh ideas for you to consider. Ideas and inspiration are everywhere; all you have to do is go looking for them.

Simply typing in "Christmas Dinner Ideas" on YouTube will yield many video suggestions. You can refine your search by specifying that you want simple recipes, vegan recipes, or recipes for making a Christmas turkey. The potential of YouTube is limitless.

It's an unexpected choice, but Facebook is a great place to find answers to issues since people ask all sorts of things on their walls and in groups and get great feedback every time.

You will surely come up with a variety of excellent ideas that you can incorporate into your celebration of the holiday by simply inquiring about the activities that other people partake in during the holiday season.

Pinterest — All of the Pinterest devotees will work together to make special Christmas dinner pinboards that you can read at your leisure. Using the right keywords for your needs, you can search. If you're looking for Thanksgiving menus other than only turkey recipes, you have options.

Grandma: You can't place too much faith in Grandma's knowledge. If you ask, she probably has some delicious dishes she'd be happy to share with you and even offer to prepare for you a written recipe, in which case you'll have to find out how to make it from her in person.

Mom – Your mom will gladly share her tried-and-true recipes with you and likely has some smart ideas for the impending holidays. When you ask around, you'll find that everyone and their mother has an original idea or two to offer.

If your holiday guest can't be with their family this year, you owe it to them to call their mom and find out what makes Christmas memorable for them and what they miss the most about being with their own family.

Talk to your pals about their favourite holiday dishes to make in the kitchen this season. People will certainly share many variations of the traditional recipes you make, but they may also suggest some new twists. This is especially true if your social circle includes people from different cultural backgrounds.

Manuals of Culinary Arts - Keep in mind that cookbooks are a valuable resource. It's still possible to come up with great ideas using these techniques. A day spent in a bookshop perusing a wide selection of recipes is a great way to kickstart your imagination.

Then, before shelling out cash for that cookbook, you can verify if your local library has a copy.

Publications for General Consumption Sooner or later, the magazine racks will be groaning under the weight of seasonal articles. If you need inspiration quickly, though, you could always peruse the publications from the prior year that are on the library's shelves.

Visit your local library to peruse back issues of your favourite magazines. Copying pages from the magazine to keep the recipes with you as you leave is usually allowed as well.

You can get inspiration from a wide variety of things. The most critical consideration, though, is to not let one's head become cluttered with too many possibilities. To avoid overcooking or undercooking the food for this important holiday dinner, it is best to assess what your goal for the evening is, set a theme of some kind, and then restrict the amount that you cook to that.

Chapter 4: Eight Delicious Substitutes for the Traditional Christmas Feast

No one can dispute the worth of customs and rituals. It's a lot of fun. Like being at home. For us humans, rituals have a special appeal because they provide a sense of stability and security.
When it comes to food, though, there's no reason to choose between tradition and innovation.

By making minor adjustments to tried-and-true recipes, you may create something new that's just as delicious as the old standbys. You can stick to tradition while adding your own unique spin on things.

We recommend the following ideas in the hopes that they may free your mind to explore new possibilities.

- Many people's Christmas feasts include turkey because it is a classic dish. Most families offer a traditional roasted turkey with stuffing or dressing. Alternatively, Rachel Ray, Every Day has featured six different flavour enhancements to the classic Thanksgiving turkey over the years. These dishes are great for satisfying your family's cravings for familiar flavours while giving them a little something extra.

- Comparing Stuffing and Dressing Whether one should make stuffing or dressing is a topic of heated controversy every Thanksgiving. Either one will do the trick, but if you really want to make it shine, try switching up the components. Numerous flavour combinations can be found to be quite delightful. Try your hand at cooking this Thanksgiving Turkey with Rice Stuffing recipe.

- Although adopting a vegan lifestyle may appear to be an insurmountable obstacle, the holiday meal you make for your loved ones might benefit greatly from the switch. The Whole Foods Market website is a great resource for tasty meal ideas. Most of the ingredients you'll need can be found at a regular grocery shop, even if there isn't a Whole Foods nearby.

- Thanksgiving Ham The spiralized glazed ham is a popular Christmas dish. It tastes fantastic fresh, but the next day's leftovers are even better.

- Numerous recipes exist for this timeless dish, and many of them produce nearly identical outcomes. Why not try this Texas-style twist on traditional Thanksgiving ham? It is available to everyone, not only Texans.

- A sweet dessert made with pumpkin You may think you've seen every variation of your favourite pumpkin pie, but there are actually many more than I've been able to list. However, if you head over to Community Table's website, you can peruse these lovely 12 takes on the classic pumpkin pie. Get ready for a period of severe hunger.

- Some individuals really hate green bean casserole, but it's obvious that many others enjoy it because it's a standard part of every Christmas meal. You could be surprised to learn how many distinct approaches there are to producing it. The next paragraphs provide a list of seven different ways to improve the flavour of this traditional holiday side dish

- The traditional giblet gravy recipe is delicious on its own, but you may spice it up if you like. Sour cream can be added to the mixture for a tangy kick and amp up the richness and creaminess. Use smoked paprika or your favourite hot sauce to give it a little extra kick. Here we have still another possibility.

- Christmas Pudding - A traditional Christmas pudding is a holiday dish that many people look forward to eating. In other words, if you're English, you know exactly what's been going on.

- Yet, immigration has made this a problem in other nations as well, the United States included. Just making it according to the traditional recipe will be a novel experience if you've never tasted it before. If you like dried fruits, eggs, and bread, you'll love this.

- Try new things and don't be afraid to fail. Pizza delivery is another option for those who wish to break with traditional Christmas fare. You shouldn't feel forced to take part in the same activity year after year if you don't want. to.

- The traditional giblet gravy recipe is delicious on its own, but you may spice it up if you like. Sour cream can be added to the mixture for a tangy kick and to amp up the richness and creaminess. Use smoked paprika or your favourite hot sauce to give it a little extra kick. Here we have still another possibility.

- Christmas Pudding - A traditional Christmas pudding is a holiday dish that many people look forward to eating. In other words, if you're English, you know exactly what's been going on.

Yet, immigration has made this a problem in other nations as well, the United States included. Just making it according to the traditional recipe will be a novel experience if you've never tasted it before. If you like dried fruits, eggs, and bread, you'll love this.

Try new things and don't be afraid to fail. Pizza delivery is another option for those who wish to break with traditional Christmas fare. You shouldn't feel forced to take part in the same activity year after year if you don't want. to.

Chapter 5: You'll find 9 scrumptious and simple dessert recipes here

When it comes to Christmas desserts, the options are practically unlimited. Pinterest likely has a myriad of examples of this for you to peruse. But how can you pick the best ones?

If the dessert you want to make falls into a broad category that has several variations, you have found the one you want to make. All you have to do is look through the available recipes and pick the one that seems the least difficult to make.

There are both totally homemade dishes and those that are prepared with store-bought ingredients and some homemade tweaks.

- Dessert fondue with chocolate Fondue parties are fun any time of the year, but they are especially fitting for the holidays due to the abundance of good cheer and celebration they provide. Many families have a tradition of doing this on Christmas Eve while watching a great film.

- Since you can dip just about anything into chocolate, make a wide variety of treats for folks to taste. If you want to save time, it's recommended that you buy dippers that have already been made and then chop them up into manageable sizes.

- Baked Goods Created From a Cake Mix These cake mix cookies are not only a cinch to whip up, but they also taste and look quite holiday-appropriate. All you need to know is to make a delicious Christmas cookie!

- The cake mix makes for a very chewy, almost disintegrating cookie. When you serve them to your loved ones for dessert, prepare to hear squeals of delight and exclamations of awe. They will quickly become loved by everyone in your household.

- There are several variations of this traditional holiday treat, which is known as a Yule Log. Everyone in the family will be amazed by the classic dish. The chocolate flavour is delicious, and it also happens to be rather attractive. You can also use a prepackaged mix if you like.

- If you're giving a food-related present, almond Roca is a nice addition. What a lovely finishing touch. Many people like to stock up on modest gifts in tins or small gift bags throughout the holidays so that they are ready for visitors (which can be purchased for one dollar each at dollar stores). Homemade Almond Roca may be much simpler to make than you think.

- Almost everyone enjoys a tasty trifle. They exude a carefree spirit and taste so smooth and delicious. Many delicious trifle recipes are available for download on the internet. Trifles, which are layered desserts, are typically presented in clear glass serving dishes so that guests may admire the dish's construction.

- A seasonal favourite, mince pies are a combination of fruit and spices like cinnamon, cloves, and nutmeg. They are also known as "minced meat" pies.

The Food Network has a recipe for a delicious mince pie with a cornmeal crust. All the Ts and Is will be dotted and crossed for you if you follow this recipe.

- Dump cake, a popular dessert, requires only three ingredients and takes seconds to prepare. To make a "Dump Cake," all of the necessary ingredients are simply dumped into a baking dish and then baked. Preparation time is short, and mistakes are easily remedied in the kitchen.

- Baked Brownie Pudding Created utilising a slow cooker - Want a sweet treat that's easy to whip up but also has the power to lift everyone's spirits?

Whether you're short on counter space or short on time, this Slow Cooker Brownie Pudding will solve all of your dessert-related problems.

- Mint chocolate chip ice cream would be the icing on the cake for this holiday dessert. Everybody and their mother will go crazy for this Pumpkin Cobbler since it's a delightfully fresh spin on the classic pumpkin dessert. It's delicious in every aspect; it's hot and gooey and full of pumpkin.

Due to its slow cooker preparation, this recipe can't be simpler or tastier than it currently is. Do you want more slow-cooker pumpkin desserts? We invite you to join us.

There's no need to stress out over the dessert course of your holiday feast. If you prefer something sweet instead, you could always stop by the grocery store and pick up a treat. If I'm being honest, no one is going to take note or care. Making sweets at home also has the added benefit of filling the house with a merry smell, so don't be hesitant to use any of these suggestions; instead, give them a try and see which one you like best.

Chapter 6: Recipes for Festive Beverages

It's a lot of fun to try out new beverages throughout the Christmas season. It's simple and quick to mix up drinks that are both kid-friendly and adult-exclusive. Just stay away from items that will take a lot of prep or cooking time.

Using concoctions that are either created or already mixed can greatly simplify the process.

- It's a festive take on the classic, and when served in clear mugs, it looks like something straight out of a Christmas card. Hot chocolate with a hint of mint Your grownups and your kids will have a great time participating.
- If you're planning on serving this to adults, you can skip the peppermint extract and just add a shot of peppermint schnapps instead.

To avoid making your guests sick by serving them raw eggs, try this amusing and risk-free method of preparing egg nog:

- True Christmas eggnog is the kind you make at home without any booze. The recipe's simplicity belies your first impressions of it.

- To prevent putting your family's health at risk by serving them raw eggs, all you have to do is mix the ingredients in a skillet and cook it. It's highly unlikely that you'll ever want to buy it again once you realise how easy it is to make and how delicious it is.

- Mulled wine is a popular alcoholic beverage in Germany. If you ever find yourself in Germany, make sure to stop by the Christkindlmarkt in Nuremberg to sample some of the best-mulled wine and other holiday treats anywhere.

Don't fret if you can't make it; instead, give this spiced wine a whirl in a slow cooker.

Although you could look up a recipe for gingerbread hot chocolate, a store-bought hot chocolate mix would work just as well. After that, you can add spices like pumpkin pie spice to the mixture to achieve the desired taste.

However, that's not the best part; this recipe is outstanding. Spiced rum could be added to the adult version for a little extra kick.

Everyone, from kids to their parents, can enjoy the Cherry Bomb because it is a non-alcoholic drink made with real cherries. In a highball glass, mix equal parts grenadine, club soda, and cherries.

- The quantity of this dish is sufficient for feeding six people. If you want to make it a more adult drink, you can add a few ounces of vodka, gin, or rum. It looks like a very significant holiday is being celebrated, with all the red and cherry decorations. Green candy canes are available and can be used as an optional garnish.

- Holiday drinks can be made even without a fully stocked bar. To enjoy the many holiday festivities you'll be attending without becoming overly exhausted or inebriated, you should pick a theme in advance and stick to it.

Chapter 7: "The Christmas Feast" Holiday Appetizers and Snacks

Did you know that for some of the holidays, all you have to do is put out a variety of snacks and appetisers instead of preparing a full meal? Most people look forward to the holiday feast with great excitement.

Frequent small meals are a great way to try new cuisines without committing fully to anyone

- Recipes for Triscuit-Based Munchies - Even though many of Martha Stewart's recommendations call for a substantial time commitment, the following appetisers are simple to make and are a great way to repurpose leftovers that are suitable for the holidays.

- You could also use a Triscuit, some tomato sauce, turkey pepperoni, and mozzarella cheese and bake it in the oven until the cheese melts. An alternative to the Triscuit is a tortilla chip.

- Baked Crescent Rolls Recipes — You know what a crescent roll is, but did you know that you can use it to make a wide variety of holiday appetisers and snacks that your family will love and ask for more of? Assembly is simple because prefabricated parts are used.

- Sausage ball eating has become practically traditional in many parts of the United States. The Bisquick Sausage Ball recipe makes them especially simple to make. They can be made milder by using regular sausage or made spicier by using hot sausage. As with many other foods, cheese is a versatile ingredient.

- If you're hosting holiday guests this year, a cheese and meat tray is a simple and elegant way to serve appetisers to your guests. Prepare a tray with assorted meats, cheeses, fruits, bread, crackers, and chutney. That settles the matter, period. You can decorate it however you like, even making your Christmas tree snack out of food.

- Balls of cheese: The steps involved in creating cheeseballs are simple. After mixing all the ingredients, form the mixture into the desired form, and chill it in the fridge for at least an hour before serving. It can add a variety of flavours to cheese, and it always makes it look more festive. Several excellent cheese ball recipes can be found on Delish.com, where you can get started.

- Eggs deviled with mayonnaise are a popular dish that can be prepared in a variety of ways, the majority of which begin with hard-boiled eggs.

- To produce a filling, you separate the yellow part of the egg and combine it with a variety of other components. This recipe is intriguing since you paint the egg whites that you have cooked to look like seasonal colours, which makes the dish even more festive.

- To answer your question, yes, you may make a delectable salad to serve as a snack or appetiser. This is because there are times when people want a break from more substantial meals even though they are still hungry. The goal is accomplished by using this recipe for Cranberry Almond Spinach Salad. To make things even simpler, you may buy the dressing already prepared.

- Apples and Date Dip - This is an incredibly simple recipe. Although a recipe is not strictly necessary, we will provide a link to one for your convenience. Dates that have been soaked and pitted are combined with water and blended until they reach the desired consistency for dipping apples, which is a smooth consistency.

To enhance the flavour of the date dip and give it a more festive feel, you may also add cinnamon to it. This is truly nutritious, and it has the flavour of caramel. Your guests are going to be blown away. A helpful hint: If you don't have a high-powered blender, soak the dates in water for several hours before blending them.

We hope that these suggestions for snacks and appetisers will inspire you to begin formulating plans for what you are going to prepare. Always take into consideration how quickly it can be made, as well as how it can be stored. Be sure to make preparations ahead of time because during the holidays, you likely already have a lot of food stored in the refrigerator.

Chapter 8: Dealing with a Variety of Nutritional Requirements

Even though the holidays are a time for indulgence, you may have family members who have certain dietary requirements that simply cannot be ignored. If this is the case for you, it is a smart idea to look for dishes that can be adapted to accommodate everyone and are prepared using products that guests can consume.

People who do not have issues related to food may not even be aware of them, but those who do will be extremely thankful for them because there is frequently nothing for them to eat, and they do not like to make a big deal out of the fact that they do not have anything to eat.

- Consider Vegan Alternatives:

If you have members of your family who are allergic to gluten and/or dairy, you may frequently discover delicious vegan options that are suitable for both dietary restrictions.

Dishes such as Gluten-Free Rice Stuffing are great options for folks who need to avoid both gluten and rice, and they also happen to be really tasty for everyone else. Since you start with rice that has not been cooked and cook it for the majority of the time in the oven, it is not even very difficult to make either:

- Please forward the menu.

If you plan on preparing a meal regardless, the best thing you can do is provide a copy of the menu with the invitation you send out. This will allow guests who are aware that they will not be able to consume the meal to respond with a "no" or contact you to discuss the possibility of bringing their dish.

Even though the food seems to be the most significant aspect of the holidays, the most important part is spending time with family and friends.

- It's a Coin Flip

You should ask everyone in the family to bring a dish to share if you are aware that enough members of your family are dealing with problems. In this manner, they will have at least one thing that they can consume.

You may offer to cook the ham or turkey (or whatever else your family eats as the main dinner), and then request guests to bring a dish that is suited to their diet.

- Use Fewer Ingredients

Those who suffer from food allergies typically have easier time-consuming dishes that have fewer ingredients. However, if you are inviting a large number of people, it is also vital to identify any items that contain ingredients like milk, eggs, and nuts, as these are some of the most prevalent foods to which persons are allergic.

At long last, try to unwind. It is impossible to satisfy everyone. You should let your guests know what you are going to give and that it is okay for them to bring something else if they are unable to eat what you have prepared. Don't single out any one person and urge that they give everything a shot.

Make everything self-serve so that individuals may make their own decisions without feeling like the spotlight is on them and the scenario.

There is nothing more miserable than having a strong craving for pumpkin pie but being aware that eating it during a huge family gathering will need several trips to the restroom as a result. Therefore, avoid pushing other people. Smile and take it with grace if they tell you "no thank you."

Chapter 9: Advanced Study Methods Hints & Helpful Advice

When you are responsible for supplying food for a large number of people, how you go about doing so will be greatly influenced by issues such as your financial condition, the state of your health, the availability of space, and the dietary selections that you and your family make.

These recommendations and advice are appropriate for any form of event, including the holiday dinner party that you are hosting.

- Establish Your Budget: It is crucial that you do this step before you begin inviting people to the event. You will likely spend, on average, ten dollars per person for the holiday meal that you will prepare.

This is vital information to have so that you can establish a budget and place a restriction on the number of participants who attend the event. You might also decide to offer the main meal and ask your guests to bring side dishes of their choosing, or you could assign specific dishes to different people if you have a particular theme that you want to stick to.

- Determine the Attendees of the Event

After you have determined how much money you have available, you can start working on the guest list. Write it down nevertheless, even if you aren't formally inviting anyone and you just plan on having your family there because that's how things have always been done.

- While you're at it, write down the names of any guests who have food allergies or dietary restrictions that you know will be attending the event. Plan Your Menu

Since you are now in the process of preparing the lunch, it is crucial that you choose if you will be cooking everything yourself or whether you can count on individuals to bring whatever you have assigned them to bring.

If you handle it in this fashion, you will be able to swiftly include the recipe that you want them to follow. You also have the option of requesting that they bring a green bean casserole and enabling them to create it according to their preferred technique.

Provide your invitees with an explanation of the protocol in order to maximise the possibility that they will follow the meal plan that has been defined for them.

- Pick Dishes That Are Easy to Prepare.

It is not a good opportunity to test out that challenging recipe you recently discovered, despite the fact that it could look to be. It is advisable to test out these recipes with your personal family rather than during a holiday dinner where there will be a huge number of visitors present.

Choose instead to make dishes that require fewer ingredients, are simpler to put together, and require less time spent on preparation.

- Think About Stocking Your Freezer With Food

At their annual holiday get-togethers, some individuals who have a freezer that is sufficiently sized like to prepare a wide variety of dishes.

They will begin loading their freezer a few weeks before the occasion, and then when it comes time to serve the meal, all they will need to do is heat it. This works incredibly well for casseroles, salad, and a range of various sorts of treats.

Remember that the visitors are there to spend time with you and the other guests since this is the most vital thing to keep in mind. They are not simply there to consume the food. You may quickly arrange a wonderful and stress-free holiday meal by offering everyone the choice to build their pizzas or by setting up a potato bar. To create a successful event, you need not stick to every single established custom to do anything.

Chapter 10: Five Options That Are Suitable for Children

Kids of all ages adore providing a hand in the kitchen. This compilation of ideas will turn you into your family's most beloved member if you involve your children or grandchildren in the process of preparing food.

These suggestions will help you get a good start in thinking about the kinds of activities youngsters appreciate.

- S'Mores are a given, as is to be expected. There is no such thing as a kid-friendly Christmas dish that does not involve s'mores in some way. The delightful flavour combination of graham crackers, marshmallows, and chocolate is a favourite among all people.

- On the other hand, were you aware that you can also make them in the oven? Allow your child to layer crackers, chocolate bar, and marshmallows in a pan, and then bake the dish at 350 degrees Fahrenheit for about ten minutes, or until the marshmallow begins to rise and the chocolate begins to melt.

- The children's all-time favourite cookie is the Holly Cookie, and it's simple to see why. They are not difficult to construct and can be done so with the assistance of an adult. They don't take a lot of ingredients, and in fact, it's conceivable that you already have most of them on hand during the holiday season. Cookies prepared with cornflakes, butter, marshmallows, and cinnamon candies are among the nicest sorts.

- House Made of Gingerbread - For some families, creating a gingerbread home is a holiday ritual; for others, it's just a pipe dream. Either way, it's a lot of fun for youngsters to construct their own gingerbread houses, which are delicious and easy to prepare. Pinterest is a terrific site to look for inventive applications of graham crackers.

- Sugar cookies are a fixture in the holiday baking of a lot of families. Sugar cookies can be prepared in a variety of ways, one of which is to use pre-made cookie dough that has been chilled.

- The most enjoyable part is decorating them. You can cook them ahead of time, and then your children can help you decorate them. These pie dough cookies made with a shortcut are the answer to simplifying your life.

- Sandwiches - Kids like sandwiches. You can set out the components for sandwiches and let youngsters build them on their own. Provide them with some cookie cutters so they can cut out designs from the sandwiches in order to make them more appropriate for the holiday. You have a wide array of alternatives for fillings, including ham, turkey, pimento cheese, and hummus.

- Food That Can Be Dipped Children like any kind of food that can be dipped, and adults do too! It is possible to create turkey nuggets and serve them with cranberry sauce for dipping.

Stuffing with bacon for the holiday of Christmas

🍴 8 servings    35 minutes    55 minutes

Introduction

Amazing food is an essential component of any successful holiday celebration. Even Christmas does not make an exception. The following is a recipe that I recommend trying out if you want to finally rid the world of stale fruit cake and dressing that has too much sage flavour. Enjoy!

Ingredients

- 8 ounces of applewood-smoked bacon, diced into pieces measuring half an inch.
- Rice:
- 4 1/2 a cup of chicken broth with a reduced salt content
- 3 teaspoons of fresh thyme, finely chopped
- 1 and a quarter cups of brown rice with short grains
- 1 and a quarter cups of wild rice
- Vegetables:
- 2 tablespoons of butter that is unsalted and at room temperature
- 2 tablespoons extra-virgin olive oil
- Pearl onions from one 14-ounce bag, frozen and then thawed
- 1 teaspoon kosher salt
- Black pepper, freshly ground, one-fourth of a teaspoon

Stuffing with bacon for the holiday of Christmas

🍴 8 servings  35 minutes  55 minutes

- Twelve ounces (3 large) portobello mushrooms that have been shredded or sliced very thinly
- Eight ounces Brussels sprouts that have been cleaned, then sliced very thinly.
- Toast the hazelnuts, remove the husks, and finely slice the hazelnuts (optional)
- 6 cloves garlic, finely chopped
- 3 strips bacon, cut into 1 inch pieces
- 3 tablespoons olive oil, divided
- 2 tablespoons balsamic vinegar
- Salt and ground black pepper to taste
- 1 tablespoon freshly grated Asiago cheese

Preparation

- In a large pan set over medium heat, cook the bacon until it is nice and crispy, about 8 to 10 minutes. The bacon should be drained on some paper towels using a slotted spoon.
- To prepare the rice, place the broth and thyme in a Dutch oven or heavy-bottomed pot and bring to a boil over medium-high heat. Mix in the wild rice and brown rice.
- Cover the saucepan and place it over low heat.

Stuffing with bacon for the holiday of Christmas

🍴 8 servings    35 minutes   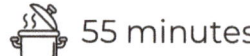 55 minutes

- Simmer for thirty minutes, or until the rice is cooked but still has some bite. Remove the pan from the heat and let the rice sit undisturbed for ten minutes.
- To fluff, use a fork.
- In the same skillet that you used to cook the bacon, melt the butter and oil over medium-high heat. Then, use the same skillet to saute the vegetables.
- After adding the onions, season them with half a teaspoon of salt and a quarter of a teaspoon of pepper.
- 1 tablespoon freshly grated Asiago cheese
- Cook for about 5 minutes, stirring regularly until the butter turns golden. Mix a quarter of a teaspoon of salt and a quarter of a teaspoon of pepper in the mushrooms.
- Cook for about 8 minutes, or until it has become more pliable. After adding the Brussels sprouts, sprinkle them with the remaining 1/4 teaspoon of salt and 1/4 teaspoon of pepper. Wait 5 minutes before serving.

Stuffing with bacon for the holiday of Christmas

🍴 8 servings  35 minutes  55 minutes

- Move the vegetable mixture into the pot with the rice once it has been cooked.
- The hazelnuts and the cooked bacon should be added.
- Mix everything by tossing it for a few moments.
- Move the mixture to a big bowl. Serve.
- Notes from the Chef: Rice can alternatively be prepared by simmering it in 4 cups of broth combined with 1/2 cup of water.
- To get a nice toasted flavour from the hazelnuts, spread them out in one layer on a baking sheet.
- Toast the almonds in an oven that has been prepared at 350 degrees Fahrenheit for about 8 to 10 minutes. Wait until it has cooled.

Fig And Orange Glazed Ham

 24 servings  5 minutes 2 hours

Introduction

Believe me when I say that I take full advantage of the fact that Christmas is the ideal time of year to overindulge in all of my favourite foods, and I encourage you to do the same. I am well aware that the majority of people look forward to sweets and baked products during this time of year; nevertheless, the ham is what excites me the most. Because there is such a wide variety of approaches to making it, it is quite difficult to get it wrong. The ham in your life that deserves a little bit extra can get it with the help of this recipe.

Ingredients

- 1 ham half cut in a spiral fashion
- 1 cup fig jam
- 2 teaspoons dijon mustard
- Orange zest, grated from one fruit
- 1/3 of a cup of freshly squeezed orange juice

Fig And Orange Glazed Ham

24 servings  5 minutes  2 hours

Preparation

- Follow the directions on the back of the ham box for how long to bake it and how hot the oven should be heated.
- Take the ham out of the oven around half an hour before the end of the time allotted for warming it.
- While everything is going on, put the jam, mustard, orange zest, and orange juice in a small saucepan and simmer it over low heat. Cook, stirring, just until the jam melts (do not boil).
- After basting the ham with half of the glaze, return it to the oven for the remaining half hour.
- Take the ham out of the oven and then spread the leftover glaze all over it with a spoon.

Fig And Orange Glazed Ham

 24 servings    5 minutes   2 hours

- Move the meat to a chopping board, and then carve it.
- This dish is both incredibly easy to make and incredibly tasty. I literally cannot wait to get going on mine.
- I hope you get as much pleasure out of it as I do.
- Alternately, one of my favourite things to do is switch out the fig jam for raspberry, just to keep things fresh and exciting.
- Feel free to make it your own by putting your spin on it and experimenting with it.
- No matter how you slice it, or in this case glaze it, ham is always tasty. It doesn't matter.

Chestnuts, pancetta, and Brussels Sprouts with Parsley and Pancetta

 6 servings 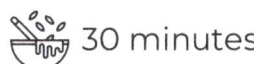 30 minutes  30 minutes

Introduction:

There are a lot of people that connect Christmas with ham, turkey, or duck, and although these are all wonderful dishes that are entirely necessary for any kind of holiday feast, let's not forget about the side dishes. The sides are like the understudies and stage managers of the production that is Christmas dinner. They are the glue that keeps your meal together and completes it. This dish for Brussels Sprouts is so incredible that it just could take the spotlight all to itself.

Ingredients

- 2 a quarter of a pound of Brussels sprouts
- 1 tablespoon vegetable oil
- 9 ounces of pancetta, with the skin, removed and the meat sliced into pieces measuring half an inch.
- Butter equivalent to 2 tablespoons
- Approximately 8 to 9 ounces of chestnuts have been vacuum-packed.
- 2 ounces of Marsala wine per fluid ounce

Chestnuts, pancetta, and Brussels Sprouts with Parsley and Pancetta

🍴 6 servings    30 minutes    30 minutes

- 1 generous handful of finely chopped fresh parsley, divided
- Black pepper that has been freshly ground

Preparation

- Remove the bases from each of the Brussels sprouts, and while you are doing so, carve a cross into the bottom of each sprout. Put the Brussels sprouts in a big saucepan and cover them with salted water. Bring the water to a boil. The Brussels sprouts should be cooked for about 5 minutes, or until they are soft but still have a bit of a bite to them.
- Take the pan from the burner and drain any extra water that has accumulated in the Brussels sprouts.
- Warm the oil in a pot that has been thoroughly cleaned.
- Pancetta cubes should be added to the pan and fried until they have a golden brown colour and a crisp texture, but they should not be cooked to the point where they have become dry.

Chestnuts, pancetta, and Brussels Sprouts with Parsley and Pancetta

6 servings 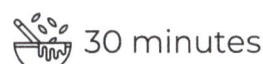 30 minutes  30 minutes

Preparation

- Put the chestnuts and butter into the pan that contains the pancetta, and then use a wooden spoon or a spatula to mash them up into smaller pieces.
- When the chestnuts have reached the desired temperature, raise the temperature of the pan and pour the Marsala into the pan.
- Continue to cook the mixture until it has decreased in volume and become somewhat thicker.
- After adding the sprouts and half of the parsley to the saucepan, ensure that everything is thoroughly combined.
- Pepper that has been freshly ground should be used to season the Brussels sprouts.
- When you are ready to serve the dish, lay the Brussels sprouts on a serving platter that has been heated, and then sprinkle the top with the remaining chopped parsley.
- This simple side dish, which manages to look gorgeous despite its ease of preparation, is destined to become a tradition at your Christmas dinner.

Gratin d'Onions Crème fraîche

🍴 8 servings    20 minutes    35 minutes

Introduction

Simply adding a casserole to any meal will make it taste ten thousand times better than it did before. There are a few exceptions to this rule, and Christmas dinner is not one of them. This buttery and creamy southern meal is so delicious that you have no choice but to make it! I hope you enjoy it as much as I do because I do.

Ingredients

- 3 kg of delicious onions (such as Vidalia, Walla Walla, or Maui onions) Sherry cream, three teaspoons' worth
- 6 tablespoons unsalted butter, split
- 1/4 cup all-purpose flour
- 1 cup of hot, scalded whole milk
- 1 cup of Parmesan cheese that has been freshly grated.
- Salt and pepper to the Kosher standard
- 1/2 cup panko crumbs

Gratin d'Onions Crème fraîche

🍴 8 servings 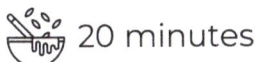 20 minutes  35 minutes

Preparation

- Turn the temperature in the oven up to 375 degrees. Prepare a gratin dish or medium casserole by greasing it with butter.
- Remove the onion's root and cut off the very tip. Peel and then cut the apple in half lengthwise.
- After cutting the onion in half lengthwise, lay the onion with the cut side down and slice it into thick wedges.
- Two tablespoons of butter should be melted over medium heat in a Dutch oven or other heavy-bottomed pot.
- After adding the onions, continue cooking them for about 40 minutes, stirring them occasionally, until they have become soft and caramelised.
- After adding the sherry, continue to boil the mixture until it has been absorbed. After removing the onions from the pan, pass the liquid through a sieve with a fine screen.

Gratin d'Onions Crème fraîche

🍴 8 servings 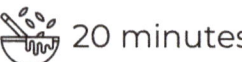 20 minutes   35 minutes

- Be patient and allow them to drain while you make the bechamel sauce. (Because the onions will continue to produce more liquid as they bake, it is necessary to drain the onions to avoid the gratin from becoming runny.)
- On a heat setting between medium and low, melt three tablespoons of butter in the Dutch oven.
- Cook for one minute after stirring in the flour, then continue cooking. After adding the scalded milk, continue cooking the sauce while whisking it continually until it reaches a fairly thick consistency.
- Take the dish away from the heat. After the Gruyere has been well melted, it should be folded in and stirred.
- Salt and pepper can be added to taste as a seasoning. After adding the onions to the cheese sauce, give everything a vigorous toss so that the onions are coated evenly. To prepare the gratin, pour the onion mixture into the dish.

Gratin d'Onions Crème fraîche

8 servings  20 minutes 35 minutes

- The remaining tablespoon of butter should be melted, then panko crumbs should be mixed in.
- Sprinkle over the onions' surface, then place in the oven and bake for about 30 minutes, or until bubbling and golden brown. To be served hot.
- Because of the incredible gooeyness and bubbliness of this dish, your guests will be begging for more of it.
- Serve with a happy heart to the people you care about to get the finest results.
- Porterhouse steak that has been broiled and served with roasted garlic and lemon.
- Have you and your loved ones grown weary of the traditional Christmas meal mainstays, such as turkey, duck, or ham? If that's the case, trying your hand at this recipe will be a delectable way to shake things up a bit. Additionally, you shouldn't be afraid of the smoke because it helps seal in the taste.

Carrot Cake

 10- servings  35 minutes  30 minutes

Introduction

Although there is no such thing as too much variety or originality, there are certain traditional desserts that are exquisite just the way they have always been prepared. A Christmas meal simply would not be the same without an incredible assortment of sweet delicacies..

Ingredients

- Cake:
- 2 cups granulated sugar
- 1 1/2 cups vegetable oil
- 4 egg
- 2 tablespoons baking soda
- 2 cups all-purpose flour
- 2 teaspoons of cinnamon in ground form
- 1 teaspoon salt 1 cup flaked coconut
- Three cups' worth of shredded carrots (about 1 pound)
- 1 cup chopped walnuts
- Cream Cheese Frosting:
- 1\s1 (8-ounce) package cream cheese, softened
- 2 sticks butter, softened
- 1 teaspoon vanilla extract
- 4 cups confectioners' sugar

Carrot Cake

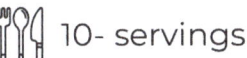 10- servings    35 minutes   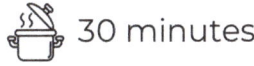 30 minutes

Preparation

- Preheat oven to 350 degrees F. Coat two 8-inch round cake pans with cooking spray; lightly flour the pans.
- In a large bowl, with an electric mixer, add granulated sugar, oil, eggs, baking soda, flour, cinnamon, salt, coconut, carrots, and walnuts, blending for 30 seconds to 1 minute, or until a homogeneous, thick mixture develops.
- DO NOT OVER-MIX! Pour batter evenly into prepared cake pans
- Bake for 45 to 50 minutes, or until a toothpick inserted in middle comes out clean and the tops are brown. Let cool fully.
- In a large bowl, with an electric mixer, create frosting by combining cream cheese and butter; beat well. Add vanilla; blend well. Gradually add confectioners' sugar, continuing to stir until fully blended.
- Place one cake layer on a serving dish and frost the top of the cake. Place the second layer on top of the frosted layer.
- Frost the top and sides of the entire cake. Serve immediately, or cover and chill until ready to serve.
- This timeless favourite is sure to please all of your sweet-toothed visitors.

Ruby Red Velvet Cake

 18 servings 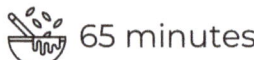 65 minutes   60 minutes

Introduction

This creamy and delicious cavalcade of savoury cream cheese frosting and fluffy
cake may have southern roots, but its exquisite flavour is cherished every Christmas nationwide. You've been nice all year, be a bit wicked with this sinfully delicious classic.

Ingredients

- 1 (18.25-ounce) packet butter-flavoured yellow cake mix
- 1/4 cup unsweetened cocoa
- 3/4 cup (1-1/2 sticks) butter, softened, divided
- 1 cup water
- 3 eggs
- 1 (1-ounce) bottle of red food colouring
- 1 1/2 cups confectioners' sugar
- 1 (8-ounce) package of cream cheese, softened
- 1 tablespoon milk

Preparation

- Preheat oven to 350 degrees F.
- Coat two 8-inch round cake pans with cooking spray.

Ruby Red Velvet Cake

 18 servings   65 minutes   🍲 60 minutes

- In a large bowl, with an electric beater on medium speed, beat cake mix, cocoa, 1/2 cup butter, water, and eggs until well blended.
- Add food colour and beat until thoroughly blended. Pour batter into prepared cake pans.
- Bake 35 to 40 minutes, or until a wooden toothpick inserted in the centre comes out clean
- Let cool for 15 minutes then invert onto a wire rack to cool completely. Using a sharp knife, carefully slice each cake in half horizontally, making a total of 4 cake layers.
- In a medium bowl, with an electric beater on medium speed, beat confectioners' sugar, cream cheese, milk, and remaining 1/4 cup butter until well blended and creamy.
- Place 1 cake layer cut-side down on a serving tray and top with 1/4 of the frosting, spreading just to the edge.
- Repeat 3 more times with remaining cake layers and icing, ending with frosting on top and leaving sides unfrosted.
- Serve, or cover loosely and chill until ready to serve.
- Nothing needs to be added to this delicacies delicious flavour except a fork and some buddies to share it with! Enjoy!

Sugar Cookies

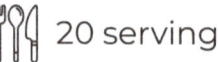 20 servings    20 minutes    10 minutes

Introduction

- We all adored these as a child, preparing them with mom on Christmas eve and decorating them for Santa. This Christmas delicacy is not only incredibly wonderful but is also tonnes of fun for the family to prepare together.

Ingredients

- 3 cups all-purpose flour
- 3/4 teaspoon baking powder
- 1/4 teaspoon salt
- 1 cup unsalted butter, softened
- 1 cup sugar
- 1 egg, beaten
- 1 tablespoon milk
- Powdered sugar, for rolling out dough

Preparation

- Sift together flour, baking powder, and salt.
- Set aside.
- Place butter and sugar in a big bowl of an electric stand mixer and beat till light in colour.

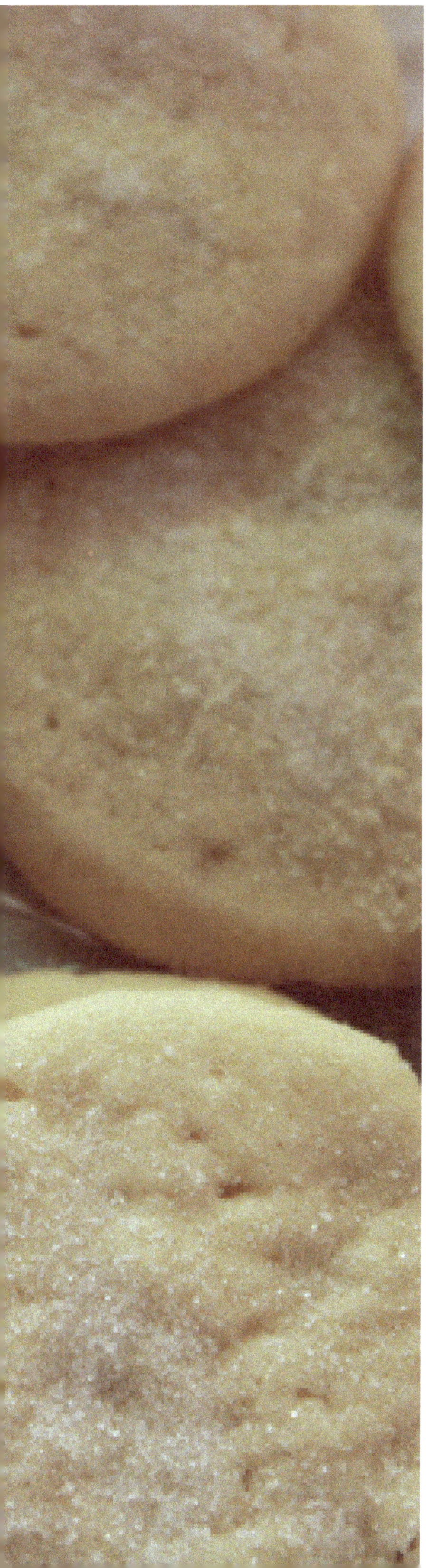

Sugar Cookies

🍴 20 servings  20 minutes  10 minutes

- Add egg and milk and whisk to mix. Put mixer on low speed, gradually add flour, and beat until mixture pulls away from the edge of the bowl.
- Divide the dough in half, wrap it in waxed paper, and refrigerate for 2 hours.
- Preheat oven to 375 degrees F.
- Sprinkle the surface where you will roll out the dough with powdered sugar.
- Remove 1 wrapped piece of dough from the refrigerator at a time, sprinkle the rolling pin with powdered sugar, and roll out the dough to 1/4-inch thick.
- Move the dough around and check underneath periodically to make sure it is not sticking.
- If the dough has warmed during rolling, place a cold cookie sheet on top for 10 minutes to chill.
- Cut into the desired shape, lay at least 1-inch apart on a greased baking sheet, parchment, or silicone baking mat, and bake for 7 to 9 minutes or until cookies are just beginning to turn brown around the edges, flipping the cookie sheet halfway through baking time.

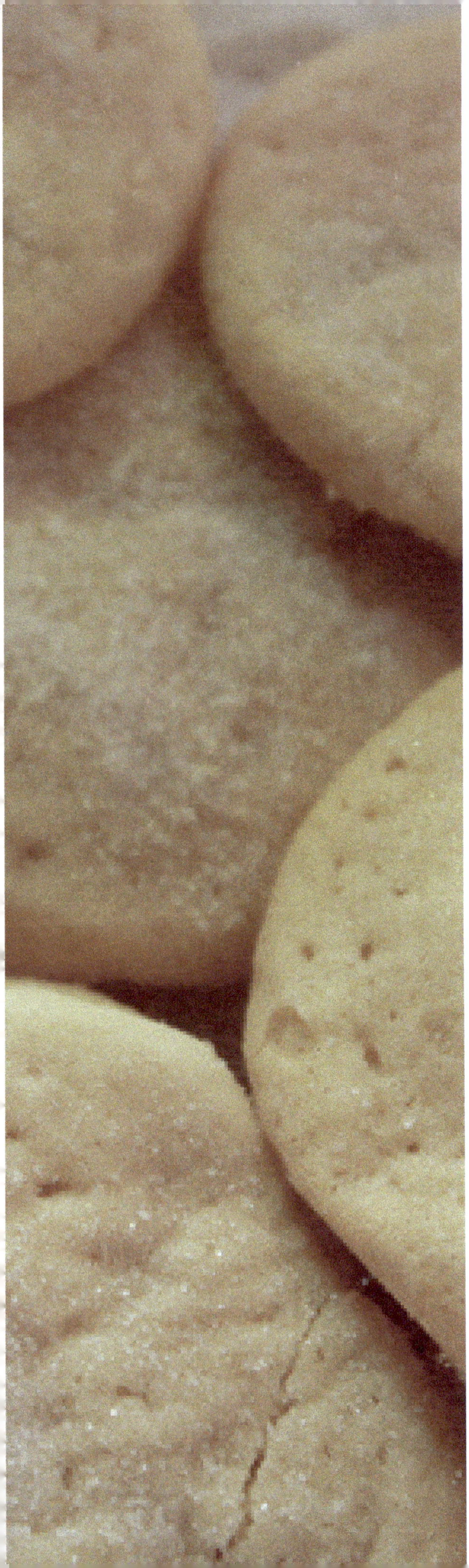

Sugar Cookies

🍴 20 servings 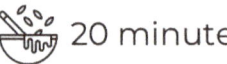 20 minutes  10 minutes

- Let rest on baking sheet for 2 minutes after removal from oven and then move to complete cooling on wire rack.
- Serve as is or ice as preferred.
- Store in an airtight container for up to 1 week.
- I recommend these cookies at Christmas time, or anytime year around.
- Frosting and decorating them is the greatest part! Have fun.

Chocolate Caramel Candy

 8 servings   45 minutes   0 minutes

Introduction

Who doesn't love getting a box of chocolates over the Christmas season? Imagine how much more it would mean to your family and friends if they were hand created by someone they love. Share this delicious meal with all those you love this year.

Ingredients

- 2 teaspoons butter
- 1 cup milk chocolate chips
- 1/4 cup butterscotch chips
- 1/4 cup creamy peanut butter
- FILLING: \s1/4 cup butter
- 1 cup sugar
- 1/4 cup evaporated milk
- 1-1/2 cups marshmallow creme
- 1/4 cup creamy peanut butter
- 1 teaspoon vanilla extract
- 1-1/2 cups chopped salted peanuts
- CARAMEL LAYER: \s1 package (14 ounces) caramels
- 1/4 cup thick whipping cream
- ICING: 1 cup (6 ounces) of milk chocolate chips
- 1/4 cup butterscotch chips
- 1/4 cup creamy peanut butter

Chocolate Caramel Candy

🍴 8 servings  45 minutes  0 minutes

Preparation

- Line a 13x9-in. pan with foil; grease foil with 2 tablespoons butter and set aside. In a small saucepan, add milk chocolate chips, butterscotch chips and peanut butter; stir over low heat until melted and smooth.
- Spread into prepared pan. Refrigerate until set.
- For the filling, in a small heavy saucepan, melt butter over medium heat. Add sugar and milk; bring to a mild boil.
- Reduce heat to medium-low; simmer and stir for 5 minutes.
- Remove from heat; mix in marshmallow crème, peanut butter and vanilla until smooth.
- Add peanuts. Spread over the first layer. Refrigerate until set.
- For the caramel layer, in a small heavy saucepan, add caramels and cream; whisk over low heat until melted and smooth.
- Cook and stir for 4 minutes. Spread over filling. Refrigerate until set.
- For frosting, in another saucepan, add chips and peanut butter; whisk over low heat until melted and smooth.

Chocolate Caramel Candy

🍴 8 servings  45 minutes  0 minutes

- Add peanuts. Spread over the first layer. Refrigerate until set.
- For the caramel layer, in a small heavy saucepan, add caramels and cream; whisk over low heat until melted and smooth.
- Cook and stir for 4 minutes. Spread over filling. Refrigerate until set.
- For frosting, in another saucepan, add chips and peanut butter; whisk over low heat until melted and smooth.
- Pour over the caramel layer. Refrigerate for at least 4 hours or overnight. Remove from the refrigerator 20 minutes before cutting.

Homemade peanut butter cups

 12 servings    25 minutes   5 minutes

Introduction

OK, so maybe it's just me, but I think chocolate and peanut butter combined is truly the most brilliant invention of man. Imagine knowing how to make your own, and being able to enjoy and share them for years to come. Sounds quite nice to me!

Ingredients

- 1 cup creamy peanut butter, divided 4-1/2 teaspoons butter, softened
- 1/2 cup confectioners' sugar
- 1/2 teaspoon salt
- 2 cups (12 ounces) semisweet chocolate chips
- 4 milk chocolate candy bars (1.55 ounces each), coarsely chopped
- Coloured sprinkles, optional

Preparation

- In a small bowl, combine 1/2 cup peanut butter, butter, confectioners' sugar and salt until smooth; set aside.
- In a microwave, melt the chocolate chips, candy bars and remaining peanut butter; stir until smooth.

Homemade peanut butter cups

🍴 12 servings   25 minutes   5 minutes

- Drop teaspoonfuls of chocolate mixture into paper-lined miniature muffin cups. Top each with a scant teaspoonful of peanut butter mixture; top with another teaspoonful of chocolate mixture.
- Decorate with sprinkles if desired. Refrigerate until set. Store in an airtight container. Yield: 3 dozen.
- These treats are so super simple and delicious, it would almost be Scroogey not to make them for your family this Christmas. You don't want to be a Grinch, do you?

Conclusion

The preparation of Christmas supper does not have to be arduous or take all night long.

You'll realise that you have a lot more fun during the holidays if you break a few traditions, choose the meals you create with care based on your budget limit and the number of people you need to serve, and consider shaking things up a bit. Keep it basic while yet making it amazing!

Have a nice Christmas!

www.ingramcontent.com/pod-product-compliance
Lightning Source LLC
Chambersburg PA
CBHW051319110526
44590CB00031B/4406